AF808037

THANK YOU FOR YOUR CONTINUED SUPPORT.

Published By My Littl' Workshop

To purchase additional
copies of this book, go to:
www.MyLittlWorkshop.com

My Littl' Workshop supports Sista Foundation Inc. a nonprofit which empowers young women and mentoring young men, and communities at large through workshops and social events.

Kakeibo Budget Book
Belongs to

____

Annual Savings Goal

$ __________

MONTH

Month by month note the savings

	$
	$
	$
	$
	$
	$
	$
	$
	$
	$
	$
	$

TOTAL $

Kakeibo budget planner

MONTH OF: /

FAMILY ACCOUNT	SAVINGS ACCOUNT
Beginning of the Month $	Beginning of the Month $

INCOME

Date: / /	Details:	Amount $
Date: / /	Details:	Amount $
Date: / /	Details:	Amount $
Date: / /	Details:	Amount $
Date: / /	Details:	Amount $
Date: / /	Details:	Amount $

TOTAL AMOUNT: $

FIXED EXPENSES

Date: / /	Details:	Amount $
Date: / /	Details:	Amount $
Date: / /	Details:	Amount $
Date: / /	Details:	Amount $
Date: / /	Details:	Amount $
Date: / /	Details:	Amount $
Date: / /	Details:	Amount $
Date: / /	Details:	Amount $
Date: / /	Details:	Amount $
Date: / /	Details:	Amount $

TOTAL AMOUNT: $

AVAILABLE MONEY

$

MONTH OF:

Weekly Goal

WEEK -

HOW MUCH I WANT TO SAVE

$

ESTIMATED SPENDING MONEY

Monday

$ $
$ $
$ $
$ $
$ $
$ $
$ $
$ $
$ $
$ $
$ $

Tuesday

$ $
$ $
$ $
$ $
$ $
$ $
$ $
$ $
$ $
$ $
$ $

Wednesday

$ $
$ $
$ $
$ $
$ $
$ $
$ $
$ $
$ $
$ $
$ $

Thursday

$ $
$ $
$ $
$ $
$ $
$ $
$ $
$ $
$ $
$ $
$ $

MONTH OF:

Weekly Goal

WEEK -

ESTIMATED SPENDING MONEY

Friday

	$	$
	$	$
	$	$
	$	$
	$	$
	$	$
	$	$
	$	$
	$	$
	$	$
	$	$

Saturday

	$	$
	$	$
	$	$
	$	$
	$	$
	$	$
	$	$
	$	$
	$	$
	$	$
	$	$

Sunday

	$	$
	$	$
	$	$
	$	$
	$	$
	$	$
	$	$
	$	$
	$	$
	$	$
	$	$

WEEKLY ESTIMATED

$ ____________

WEEKLY EXPENSES

$ ____________

=

MONTH OF:

Weekly Goal

WEEK -

HOW MUCH I WANT TO SAVE

$

ESTIMATED SPENDING MONEY

Monday

$ $
$ $
$ $
$ $
$ $
$ $
$ $
$ $
$ $
$ $
$ $

Tuesday

$ $
$ $
$ $
$ $
$ $
$ $
$ $
$ $
$ $
$ $
$ $

Wednesday

$ $
$ $
$ $
$ $
$ $
$ $
$ $
$ $
$ $
$ $
$ $

Thursday

$ $
$ $
$ $
$ $
$ $
$ $
$ $
$ $
$ $
$ $
$ $

MONTH OF:

Weekly Goal

WEEK -

ESTIMATED SPENDING MONEY

Friday

	$	$
	$	$
	$	$
	$	$
	$	$
	$	$
	$	$
	$	$
	$	$
	$	$
	$	$

Saturday

	$	$
	$	$
	$	$
	$	$
	$	$
	$	$
	$	$
	$	$
	$	$
	$	$
	$	$

Sunday

	$	$
	$	$
	$	$
	$	$
	$	$
	$	$
	$	$
	$	$
	$	$
	$	$
	$	$

WEEKLY ESTIMATED

$

WEEKLY EXPENSES

$

=

MONTH OF:

Weekly Goal

WEEK -

HOW MUCH I WANT TO SAVE

$

ESTIMATED SPENDING MONEY

Monday

	$	$
	$	$
	$	$
	$	$
	$	$
	$	$
	$	$
	$	$
	$	$
	$	$
	$	$

Tuesday

	$	$
	$	$
	$	$
	$	$
	$	$
	$	$
	$	$
	$	$
	$	$
	$	$
	$	$

Wednesday

	$	$
	$	$
	$	$
	$	$
	$	$
	$	$
	$	$
	$	$
	$	$
	$	$
	$	$

Thursday

	$	$
	$	$
	$	$
	$	$
	$	$
	$	$
	$	$
	$	$
	$	$
	$	$
	$	$

MONTH OF:

Weekly Goal

WEEK -

ESTIMATED SPENDING MONEY

Friday

☐ ☐ ☐

	$	$
	$	$
	$	$
	$	$
	$	$
	$	$
	$	$
	$	$
	$	$
	$	$
	$	$

Saturday

☐ ☐ ☐

	$	$
	$	$
	$	$
	$	$
	$	$
	$	$
	$	$
	$	$
	$	$
	$	$
	$	$

Sunday

☐ ☐ ☐

	$	$
	$	$
	$	$
	$	$
	$	$
	$	$
	$	$
	$	$
	$	$
	$	$
	$	$

WEEKLY ESTIMATED

$

WEEKLY EXPENSES

$

=

Weekly Savings

$

MONTH OF:

Weekly Goal

WEEK -

HOW MUCH I WANT TO SAVE

$

ESTIMATED SPENDING MONEY

Monday

$ $
$ $
$ $
$ $
$ $
$ $
$ $
$ $
$ $
$ $
$ $

Tuesday

$ $
$ $
$ $
$ $
$ $
$ $
$ $
$ $
$ $
$ $
$ $

Wednesday

$ $
$ $
$ $
$ $
$ $
$ $
$ $
$ $
$ $
$ $
$ $

Thursday

$ $
$ $
$ $
$ $
$ $
$ $
$ $
$ $
$ $
$ $
$ $

MONTH OF:

Weekly Goal

WEEK -

ESTIMATED SPENDING MONEY

Friday

☐ ☐ ☐

	$	$
	$	$
	$	$
	$	$
	$	$
	$	$
	$	$
	$	$
	$	$
	$	$
	$	$

Saturday

☐ ☐ ☐

	$	$
	$	$
	$	$
	$	$
	$	$
	$	$
	$	$
	$	$
	$	$
	$	$
	$	$

Sunday

☐ ☐ ☐

	$	$
	$	$
	$	$
	$	$
	$	$
	$	$
	$	$
	$	$
	$	$
	$	$
	$	$

WEEKLY ESTIMATED

$ ______

WEEKLY EXPENSES

$ ______

=

Expense Tracker

DATE:	CATEGORY	AMOUNT
/ /		$
/ /		$
/ /		$
/ /		$
/ /		$
/ /		$
/ /		$
/ /		$
/ /		$
/ /		$
/ /		$
/ /		$
/ /		$
/ /		$
/ /		$
/ /		$
/ /		$
/ /		$
/ /		$
/ /		$
/ /		$
/ /		$
/ /		$
	TOTAL SPENDING	$

Monthly Balance Chart

TOTAL EXPENSES

CATEGORY

1. $ ____________
2. $ ____________
3. $ ____________
4. $ ____________

FIXED EXPENSES $ ____________

TOTAL EXPENSES $ ____________

SPENDING CIRCLE CHART

TOTAL INCOME $ ____________

TOTAL EXPENSES $ ____________

MONTHLY SAVE $ ____________

IMPORTANT NOTES

Special Notes

Kakeibo budget planner

MONTH OF: /

FAMILY ACCOUNT	SAVINGS ACCOUNT
Beginning of the Month $	Beginning of the Month $

INCOME

Date: / /	Details:	Amount $
Date: / /	Details:	Amount $
Date: / /	Details:	Amount $
Date: / /	Details:	Amount $
Date: / /	Details:	Amount $
Date: / /	Details:	Amount $

TOTAL AMOUNT: $

FIXED EXPENSES

Date: / /	Details:	Amount $
Date: / /	Details:	Amount $
Date: / /	Details:	Amount $
Date: / /	Details:	Amount $
Date: / /	Details:	Amount $
Date: / /	Details:	Amount $
Date: / /	Details:	Amount $
Date: / /	Details:	Amount $
Date: / /	Details:	Amount $
Date: / /	Details:	Amount $

TOTAL AMOUNT: $

AVAILABLE MONEY

$

MONTH OF:

Weekly Goal

WEEK -

HOW MUCH I WANT TO SAVE

$

ESTIMATED SPENDING MONEY

Monday

	$	$
	$	$
	$	$
	$	$
	$	$
	$	$
	$	$
	$	$
	$	$
	$	$
	$	$

Tuesday

	$	$
	$	$
	$	$
	$	$
	$	$
	$	$
	$	$
	$	$
	$	$
	$	$
	$	$

Wednesday

	$	$
	$	$
	$	$
	$	$
	$	$
	$	$
	$	$
	$	$
	$	$
	$	$
	$	$

Thursday

	$	$
	$	$
	$	$
	$	$
	$	$
	$	$
	$	$
	$	$
	$	$
	$	$
	$	$

MONTH OF:

Weekly Goal

WEEK -

ESTIMATED SPENDING MONEY

Friday

	$	$
	$	$
	$	$
	$	$
	$	$
	$	$
	$	$
	$	$
	$	$
	$	$
	$	$

Saturday

	$	$
	$	$
	$	$
	$	$
	$	$
	$	$
	$	$
	$	$
	$	$
	$	$
	$	$

Sunday

	$	$
	$	$
	$	$
	$	$
	$	$
	$	$
	$	$
	$	$
	$	$
	$	$
	$	$

WEEKLY ESTIMATED

$ ____________

WEEKLY EXPENSES

$ ____________

=

MONTH OF:

Weekly Goal

WEEK -

HOW MUCH I WANT TO SAVE

$

ESTIMATED SPENDING MONEY

Monday

	$	$
	$	$
	$	$
	$	$
	$	$
	$	$
	$	$
	$	$
	$	$
	$	$
	$	$

Tuesday

	$	$
	$	$
	$	$
	$	$
	$	$
	$	$
	$	$
	$	$
	$	$
	$	$
	$	$

Wednesday

	$	$
	$	$
	$	$
	$	$
	$	$
	$	$
	$	$
	$	$
	$	$
	$	$
	$	$

Thursday

	$	$
	$	$
	$	$
	$	$
	$	$
	$	$
	$	$
	$	$
	$	$
	$	$
	$	$

MONTH OF:

Weekly Goal

WEEK -

ESTIMATED SPENDING MONEY

Friday

☐ ☐ ☐

	$	$
	$	$
	$	$
	$	$
	$	$
	$	$
	$	$
	$	$
	$	$
	$	$
	$	$

Saturday

☐ ☐ ☐

	$	$
	$	$
	$	$
	$	$
	$	$
	$	$
	$	$
	$	$
	$	$
	$	$
	$	$

Sunday

☐ ☐ ☐

	$	$
	$	$
	$	$
	$	$
	$	$
	$	$
	$	$
	$	$
	$	$
	$	$
	$	$

WEEKLY ESTIMATED

$ ____________

WEEKLY EXPENSES

$ ____________

=

MONTH OF:

Weekly Goal

WEEK -

HOW MUCH I WANT TO SAVE

$

ESTIMATED SPENDING MONEY

Monday

	$	$
	$	$
	$	$
	$	$
	$	$
	$	$
	$	$
	$	$
	$	$
	$	$
	$	$

Tuesday

	$	$
	$	$
	$	$
	$	$
	$	$
	$	$
	$	$
	$	$
	$	$
	$	$
	$	$

Wednesday

	$	$
	$	$
	$	$
	$	$
	$	$
	$	$
	$	$
	$	$
	$	$
	$	$
	$	$

Thursday

	$	$
	$	$
	$	$
	$	$
	$	$
	$	$
	$	$
	$	$
	$	$
	$	$
	$	$

MONTH OF:

Weekly Goal

WEEK -

ESTIMATED SPENDING MONEY

Friday

	$	$
	$	$
	$	$
	$	$
	$	$
	$	$
	$	$
	$	$
	$	$
	$	$
	$	$

Saturday

	$	$
	$	$
	$	$
	$	$
	$	$
	$	$
	$	$
	$	$
	$	$
	$	$
	$	$

Sunday

	$	$
	$	$
	$	$
	$	$
	$	$
	$	$
	$	$
	$	$
	$	$
	$	$
	$	$

WEEKLY ESTIMATED

$ ______

WEEKLY EXPENSES

$ ______

=

MONTH OF:

Weekly Goal

WEEK -

HOW MUCH I WANT TO SAVE

$

ESTIMATED SPENDING MONEY

Monday

	$	$
	$	$
	$	$
	$	$
	$	$
	$	$
	$	$
	$	$
	$	$
	$	$
	$	$

Tuesday

	$	$
	$	$
	$	$
	$	$
	$	$
	$	$
	$	$
	$	$
	$	$
	$	$
	$	$

Wednesday

	$	$
	$	$
	$	$
	$	$
	$	$
	$	$
	$	$
	$	$
	$	$
	$	$
	$	$

Thursday

	$	$
	$	$
	$	$
	$	$
	$	$
	$	$
	$	$
	$	$
	$	$
	$	$
	$	$

MONTH OF:

Weekly Goal

WEEK -

ESTIMATED SPENDING MONEY

Friday

	$	$
	$	$
	$	$
	$	$
	$	$
	$	$
	$	$
	$	$
	$	$
	$	$
	$	$
	$	$

Saturday

	$	$
	$	$
	$	$
	$	$
	$	$
	$	$
	$	$
	$	$
	$	$
	$	$
	$	$
	$	$

Sunday

	$	$
	$	$
	$	$
	$	$
	$	$
	$	$
	$	$
	$	$
	$	$
	$	$
	$	$
	$	$

WEEKLY ESTIMATED

$ __________

WEEKLY EXPENSES

$ __________

=

Weekly Savings

$ __________

Expense Tracker

DATE:	CATEGORY	AMOUNT
/ /		$
/ /		$
/ /		$
/ /		$
/ /		$
/ /		$
/ /		$
/ /		$
/ /		$
/ /		$
/ /		$
/ /		$
/ /		$
/ /		$
/ /		$
/ /		$
/ /		$
/ /		$
/ /		$
/ /		$
/ /		$
/ /		$
/ /		$
	TOTAL SPENDING	$

Monthly Balance Chart

TOTAL EXPENSES

CATEGORY	SPENDING CIRCLE CHART

1. $ ____________
2. $ ____________
3. $ ____________
4. $ ____________

FIXED EXPENSES $ ____________

TOTAL EXPENSES $ ____________

TOTAL INCOME $ ____________

TOTAL EXPENSES $ ____________

MONTHLY SAVE $ ____________

IMPORTANT NOTES

Special Notes

Kakeibo budget planner

MONTH OF: /

FAMILY ACCOUNT	SAVINGS ACCOUNT
Beginning of the Month $	Beginning of the Month $

INCOME

Date: / /	Details:	Amount $
Date: / /	Details:	Amount $
Date: / /	Details:	Amount $
Date: / /	Details:	Amount $
Date: / /	Details:	Amount $
Date: / /	Details:	Amount $

TOTAL AMOUNT: $

FIXED EXPENSES

Date: / /	Details:	Amount $
Date: / /	Details:	Amount $
Date: / /	Details:	Amount $
Date: / /	Details:	Amount $
Date: / /	Details:	Amount $
Date: / /	Details:	Amount $
Date: / /	Details:	Amount $
Date: / /	Details:	Amount $
Date: / /	Details:	Amount $
Date: / /	Details:	Amount $

TOTAL AMOUNT: $

AVAILABLE MONEY

$

MONTH OF:

Weekly Goal

WEEK -

HOW MUCH I WANT TO SAVE

$

ESTIMATED SPENDING MONEY

Monday

	$	$
	$	$
	$	$
	$	$
	$	$
	$	$
	$	$
	$	$
	$	$
	$	$
	$	$

Tuesday

	$	$
	$	$
	$	$
	$	$
	$	$
	$	$
	$	$
	$	$
	$	$
	$	$
	$	$

Wednesday

	$	$
	$	$
	$	$
	$	$
	$	$
	$	$
	$	$
	$	$
	$	$
	$	$
	$	$

Thursday

	$	$
	$	$
	$	$
	$	$
	$	$
	$	$
	$	$
	$	$
	$	$
	$	$
	$	$

MONTH OF:

Weekly Goal

WEEK -

ESTIMATED SPENDING MONEY

Friday

	$	$
	$	$
	$	$
	$	$
	$	$
	$	$
	$	$
	$	$
	$	$
	$	$
	$	$

Saturday

	$	$
	$	$
	$	$
	$	$
	$	$
	$	$
	$	$
	$	$
	$	$
	$	$
	$	$

Sunday

	$	$
	$	$
	$	$
	$	$
	$	$
	$	$
	$	$
	$	$
	$	$
	$	$
	$	$

WEEKLY ESTIMATED

$ ____________

WEEKLY EXPENSES

$ ____________

=

MONTH OF:

Weekly Goal

WEEK -

HOW MUCH I WANT TO SAVE

$

ESTIMATED SPENDING MONEY

Monday

	$	$
	$	$
	$	$
	$	$
	$	$
	$	$
	$	$
	$	$
	$	$
	$	$
	$	$

Tuesday

	$	$
	$	$
	$	$
	$	$
	$	$
	$	$
	$	$
	$	$
	$	$
	$	$
	$	$

Wednesday

	$	$
	$	$
	$	$
	$	$
	$	$
	$	$
	$	$
	$	$
	$	$
	$	$
	$	$

Thursday

	$	$
	$	$
	$	$
	$	$
	$	$
	$	$
	$	$
	$	$
	$	$
	$	$
	$	$

MONTH OF:

Weekly Goal

WEEK -

ESTIMATED SPENDING MONEY

Friday

☐ ☐ ☐

	$	$
	$	$
	$	$
	$	$
	$	$
	$	$
	$	$
	$	$
	$	$
	$	$
	$	$

Saturday

☐ ☐ ☐

	$	$
	$	$
	$	$
	$	$
	$	$
	$	$
	$	$
	$	$
	$	$
	$	$
	$	$

Sunday

☐ ☐ ☐

	$	$
	$	$
	$	$
	$	$
	$	$
	$	$
	$	$
	$	$
	$	$
	$	$
	$	$

WEEKLY ESTIMATED

$ ____________

WEEKLY EXPENSES

$ ____________

=

Weekly Savings

$ ____________

MONTH OF:

Weekly Goal

WEEK -

HOW MUCH I WANT TO SAVE

$

ESTIMATED SPENDING MONEY

Monday

$ $
$ $
$ $
$ $
$ $
$ $
$ $
$ $
$ $
$ $
$ $

Tuesday

$ $
$ $
$ $
$ $
$ $
$ $
$ $
$ $
$ $
$ $
$ $

Wednesday

$ $
$ $
$ $
$ $
$ $
$ $
$ $
$ $
$ $
$ $
$ $

Thursday

$ $
$ $
$ $
$ $
$ $
$ $
$ $
$ $
$ $
$ $
$ $

MONTH OF:

Weekly Goal

WEEK -

ESTIMATED SPENDING MONEY

Friday

☐ ☐ ☐

	$	$
	$	$
	$	$
	$	$
	$	$
	$	$
	$	$
	$	$
	$	$
	$	$
	$	$

Saturday

☐ ☐ ☐

	$	$
	$	$
	$	$
	$	$
	$	$
	$	$
	$	$
	$	$
	$	$
	$	$
	$	$

Sunday

☐ ☐ ☐

	$	$
	$	$
	$	$
	$	$
	$	$
	$	$
	$	$
	$	$
	$	$
	$	$
	$	$

WEEKLY ESTIMATED

$ ____________

WEEKLY EXPENSES

$ ____________

=

MONTH OF:

Weekly Goal

WEEK -

HOW MUCH I WANT TO SAVE

$

ESTIMATED SPENDING MONEY

Monday

☐ ☐ ☐

	$	$
	$	$
	$	$
	$	$
	$	$
	$	$
	$	$
	$	$
	$	$
	$	$
	$	$

Tuesday

☐ ☐ ☐

	$	$
	$	$
	$	$
	$	$
	$	$
	$	$
	$	$
	$	$
	$	$
	$	$
	$	$

Wednesday

☐ ☐ ☐

	$	$
	$	$
	$	$
	$	$
	$	$
	$	$
	$	$
	$	$
	$	$
	$	$
	$	$

Thursday

☐ ☐ ☐

	$	$
	$	$
	$	$
	$	$
	$	$
	$	$
	$	$
	$	$
	$	$
	$	$
	$	$

MONTH OF:

Weekly Goal

WEEK -

ESTIMATED SPENDING MONEY

Friday

☐ ☐ ☐

	$	$
	$	$
	$	$
	$	$
	$	$
	$	$
	$	$
	$	$
	$	$
	$	$
	$	$

Saturday

☐ ☐ ☐

	$	$
	$	$
	$	$
	$	$
	$	$
	$	$
	$	$
	$	$
	$	$
	$	$
	$	$

Sunday

☐ ☐ ☐

	$	$
	$	$
	$	$
	$	$
	$	$
	$	$
	$	$
	$	$
	$	$
	$	$
	$	$

WEEKLY ESTIMATED

$ ____________

WEEKLY EXPENSES

$ ____________

=

Weekly Savings

$ ____________

Expense Tracker

DATE:	CATEGORY	AMOUNT
/ /		$
/ /		$
/ /		$
/ /		$
/ /		$
/ /		$
/ /		$
/ /		$
/ /		$
/ /		$
/ /		$
/ /		$
/ /		$
/ /		$
/ /		$
/ /		$
/ /		$
/ /		$
/ /		$
/ /		$
/ /		$
/ /		$
/ /		$
	TOTAL SPENDING	$

Monthly Balance Chart

TOTAL EXPENSES

CATEGORY	SPENDING CIRCLE CHART

1. $ ____________
2. $ ____________
3. $ ____________
4. $ ____________

FIXED EXPENSES $ ____________

TOTAL EXPENSES $ ____________

TOTAL INCOME $ ____________

TOTAL EXPENSES $ ____________

MONTHLY SAVE $ ____________

IMPORTANT NOTES

Special Notes

Kakeibo budget planner

MONTH OF: /

FAMILY ACCOUNT	SAVINGS ACCOUNT
Beginning of the Month $	Beginning of the Month $

INCOME

Date: / /	Details:	Amount $
Date: / /	Details:	Amount $
Date: / /	Details:	Amount $
Date: / /	Details:	Amount $
Date: / /	Details:	Amount $
Date: / /	Details:	Amount $

TOTAL AMOUNT: $

FIXED EXPENSES

Date: / /	Details:	Amount $
Date: / /	Details:	Amount $
Date: / /	Details:	Amount $
Date: / /	Details:	Amount $
Date: / /	Details:	Amount $
Date: / /	Details:	Amount $
Date: / /	Details:	Amount $
Date: / /	Details:	Amount $
Date: / /	Details:	Amount $
Date: / /	Details:	Amount $

TOTAL AMOUNT: $

AVAILABLE MONEY

$

MONTH OF:

Weekly Goal

WEEK -

HOW MUCH I WANT TO SAVE

$

ESTIMATED SPENDING MONEY

Monday

	$	$
	$	$
	$	$
	$	$
	$	$
	$	$
	$	$
	$	$
	$	$
	$	$
	$	$

Tuesday

	$	$
	$	$
	$	$
	$	$
	$	$
	$	$
	$	$
	$	$
	$	$
	$	$
	$	$

Wednesday

	$	$
	$	$
	$	$
	$	$
	$	$
	$	$
	$	$
	$	$
	$	$
	$	$
	$	$

Thursday

	$	$
	$	$
	$	$
	$	$
	$	$
	$	$
	$	$
	$	$
	$	$
	$	$
	$	$

MONTH OF:

Weekly Goal

WEEK -

ESTIMATED SPENDING MONEY

Friday

	$	$
	$	$
	$	$
	$	$
	$	$
	$	$
	$	$
	$	$
	$	$
	$	$
	$	$

Saturday

	$	$
	$	$
	$	$
	$	$
	$	$
	$	$
	$	$
	$	$
	$	$
	$	$
	$	$

Sunday

	$	$
	$	$
	$	$
	$	$
	$	$
	$	$
	$	$
	$	$
	$	$
	$	$
	$	$

WEEKLY ESTIMATED

$ ________

WEEKLY EXPENSES

$ ________

=

Weekly Savings

$ ________

MONTH OF:

Weekly Goal

WEEK -

HOW MUCH I WANT TO SAVE

$

ESTIMATED SPENDING MONEY

Monday

	$	$
	$	$
	$	$
	$	$
	$	$
	$	$
	$	$
	$	$
	$	$
	$	$
	$	$

Tuesday

	$	$
	$	$
	$	$
	$	$
	$	$
	$	$
	$	$
	$	$
	$	$
	$	$
	$	$

Wednesday

	$	$
	$	$
	$	$
	$	$
	$	$
	$	$
	$	$
	$	$
	$	$
	$	$
	$	$

Thursday

	$	$
	$	$
	$	$
	$	$
	$	$
	$	$
	$	$
	$	$
	$	$
	$	$
	$	$

MONTH OF:

Weekly Goal

WEEK -

ESTIMATED SPENDING MONEY

Friday

	$	$
	$	$
	$	$
	$	$
	$	$
	$	$
	$	$
	$	$
	$	$
	$	$
	$	$

Saturday

	$	$
	$	$
	$	$
	$	$
	$	$
	$	$
	$	$
	$	$
	$	$
	$	$
	$	$

Sunday

	$	$
	$	$
	$	$
	$	$
	$	$
	$	$
	$	$
	$	$
	$	$
	$	$
	$	$

WEEKLY ESTIMATED

$ ____________

WEEKLY EXPENSES

$ ____________

=

MONTH OF:

Weekly Goal

WEEK -

HOW MUCH I WANT TO SAVE

$

ESTIMATED SPENDING MONEY

Monday

	$	$
	$	$
	$	$
	$	$
	$	$
	$	$
	$	$
	$	$
	$	$
	$	$
	$	$

Tuesday

	$	$
	$	$
	$	$
	$	$
	$	$
	$	$
	$	$
	$	$
	$	$
	$	$
	$	$

Wednesday

	$	$
	$	$
	$	$
	$	$
	$	$
	$	$
	$	$
	$	$
	$	$
	$	$
	$	$

Thursday

	$	$
	$	$
	$	$
	$	$
	$	$
	$	$
	$	$
	$	$
	$	$
	$	$
	$	$

MONTH OF:

Weekly Goal

WEEK -

ESTIMATED SPENDING MONEY

Friday

	$	$
	$	$
	$	$
	$	$
	$	$
	$	$
	$	$
	$	$
	$	$
	$	$
	$	$

Saturday

	$	$
	$	$
	$	$
	$	$
	$	$
	$	$
	$	$
	$	$
	$	$
	$	$
	$	$

Sunday

	$	$
	$	$
	$	$
	$	$
	$	$
	$	$
	$	$
	$	$
	$	$
	$	$
	$	$

WEEKLY ESTIMATED

$ ____________

WEEKLY EXPENSES

$ ____________

=

Weekly Savings

$ ____________

MONTH OF:

Weekly Goal

WEEK -

HOW MUCH I WANT TO SAVE

$

ESTIMATED SPENDING MONEY

Monday

	$	$
	$	$
	$	$
	$	$
	$	$
	$	$
	$	$
	$	$
	$	$
	$	$
	$	$

Tuesday

	$	$
	$	$
	$	$
	$	$
	$	$
	$	$
	$	$
	$	$
	$	$
	$	$
	$	$

Wednesday

	$	$
	$	$
	$	$
	$	$
	$	$
	$	$
	$	$
	$	$
	$	$
	$	$
	$	$

Thursday

	$	$
	$	$
	$	$
	$	$
	$	$
	$	$
	$	$
	$	$
	$	$
	$	$
	$	$

MONTH OF:

Weekly Goal

WEEK -

ESTIMATED SPENDING MONEY

Friday

☐ ☐ ☐

	$	$
	$	$
	$	$
	$	$
	$	$
	$	$
	$	$
	$	$
	$	$
	$	$
	$	$

Saturday

☐ ☐ ☐

	$	$
	$	$
	$	$
	$	$
	$	$
	$	$
	$	$
	$	$
	$	$
	$	$
	$	$

Sunday

☐ ☐ ☐

	$	$
	$	$
	$	$
	$	$
	$	$
	$	$
	$	$
	$	$
	$	$
	$	$
	$	$

WEEKLY ESTIMATED

$ ____________

WEEKLY EXPENSES

$ ____________

=

Weekly Savings

$ ____________

Expense Tracker

DATE:	CATEGORY	AMOUNT
/ /		$
/ /		$
/ /		$
/ /		$
/ /		$
/ /		$
/ /		$
/ /		$
/ /		$
/ /		$
/ /		$
/ /		$
/ /		$
/ /		$
/ /		$
/ /		$
/ /		$
/ /		$
/ /		$
/ /		$
/ /		$
/ /		$
/ /		$
	TOTAL SPENDING	$

Monthly Balance Chart

TOTAL EXPENSES

CATEGORY	SPENDING CIRCLE CHART

1. $ ______
2. $ ______
3. $ ______
4. $ ______

FIXED EXPENSES $ ______

TOTAL EXPENSES $ ______

TOTAL INCOME $ ______

TOTAL EXPENSES $ ______

MONTHLY SAVE $ ______

IMPORTANT NOTES

Special Notes

Kakeibo budget planner

MONTH OF: /

FAMILY ACCOUNT	SAVINGS ACCOUNT
Beginning of the Month $	Beginning of the Month $

INCOME

Date: / /	Details:	Amount $
Date: / /	Details:	Amount $
Date: / /	Details:	Amount $
Date: / /	Details:	Amount $
Date: / /	Details:	Amount $
Date: / /	Details:	Amount $

TOTAL AMOUNT: $

FIXED EXPENSES

Date: / /	Details:	Amount $
Date: / /	Details:	Amount $
Date: / /	Details:	Amount $
Date: / /	Details:	Amount $
Date: / /	Details:	Amount $
Date: / /	Details:	Amount $
Date: / /	Details:	Amount $
Date: / /	Details:	Amount $
Date: / /	Details:	Amount $
Date: / /	Details:	Amount $

TOTAL AMOUNT: $

AVAILABLE MONEY

$

MONTH OF:

Weekly Goal

WEEK -

HOW MUCH I WANT TO SAVE

$

ESTIMATED SPENDING MONEY

Monday

	$	$
	$	$
	$	$
	$	$
	$	$
	$	$
	$	$
	$	$
	$	$
	$	$
	$	$

Tuesday

	$	$
	$	$
	$	$
	$	$
	$	$
	$	$
	$	$
	$	$
	$	$
	$	$
	$	$

Wednesday

	$	$
	$	$
	$	$
	$	$
	$	$
	$	$
	$	$
	$	$
	$	$
	$	$
	$	$

Thursday

	$	$
	$	$
	$	$
	$	$
	$	$
	$	$
	$	$
	$	$
	$	$
	$	$
	$	$

MONTH OF:

Weekly Goal

WEEK -

ESTIMATED SPENDING MONEY

Friday

☐ ☐ ☐

	$	$
	$	$
	$	$
	$	$
	$	$
	$	$
	$	$
	$	$
	$	$
	$	$
	$	$

Saturday

☐ ☐ ☐

	$	$
	$	$
	$	$
	$	$
	$	$
	$	$
	$	$
	$	$
	$	$
	$	$
	$	$

Sunday

☐ ☐ ☐

	$	$
	$	$
	$	$
	$	$
	$	$
	$	$
	$	$
	$	$
	$	$
	$	$
	$	$

WEEKLY ESTIMATED

$ ____________

WEEKLY EXPENSES

$ ____________

=

MONTH OF:

Weekly Goal

WEEK -

HOW MUCH I WANT TO SAVE

$

ESTIMATED SPENDING MONEY

Monday

☐ ☐ ☐

	$	$
	$	$
	$	$
	$	$
	$	$
	$	$
	$	$
	$	$
	$	$
	$	$
	$	$

Tuesday

☐ ☐ ☐

	$	$
	$	$
	$	$
	$	$
	$	$
	$	$
	$	$
	$	$
	$	$
	$	$
	$	$

Wednesday

☐ ☐ ☐

	$	$
	$	$
	$	$
	$	$
	$	$
	$	$
	$	$
	$	$
	$	$
	$	$
	$	$

Thursday

☐ ☐ ☐

	$	$
	$	$
	$	$
	$	$
	$	$
	$	$
	$	$
	$	$
	$	$
	$	$
	$	$

MONTH OF:

Weekly Goal

WEEK -

ESTIMATED SPENDING MONEY

Friday

☐ ☐ ☐

	$	$
	$	$
	$	$
	$	$
	$	$
	$	$
	$	$
	$	$
	$	$
	$	$
	$	$

Saturday

☐ ☐ ☐

	$	$
	$	$
	$	$
	$	$
	$	$
	$	$
	$	$
	$	$
	$	$
	$	$
	$	$

Sunday

☐ ☐ ☐

	$	$
	$	$
	$	$
	$	$
	$	$
	$	$
	$	$
	$	$
	$	$
	$	$
	$	$

WEEKLY ESTIMATED

$ ____________

WEEKLY EXPENSES

$ ____________

=

Weekly Savings

$ ____________

MONTH OF:

Weekly Goal

WEEK -

HOW MUCH I WANT TO SAVE

$

ESTIMATED SPENDING MONEY

Monday

	$	$
	$	$
	$	$
	$	$
	$	$
	$	$
	$	$
	$	$
	$	$
	$	$
	$	$

Tuesday

	$	$
	$	$
	$	$
	$	$
	$	$
	$	$
	$	$
	$	$
	$	$
	$	$
	$	$

Wednesday

	$	$
	$	$
	$	$
	$	$
	$	$
	$	$
	$	$
	$	$
	$	$
	$	$
	$	$

Thursday

	$	$
	$	$
	$	$
	$	$
	$	$
	$	$
	$	$
	$	$
	$	$
	$	$
	$	$

MONTH OF:

Weekly Goal

WEEK -

ESTIMATED SPENDING MONEY

Friday

☐ ☐ ☐

	$	$
	$	$
	$	$
	$	$
	$	$
	$	$
	$	$
	$	$
	$	$
	$	$
	$	$

Saturday

☐ ☐ ☐

	$	$
	$	$
	$	$
	$	$
	$	$
	$	$
	$	$
	$	$
	$	$
	$	$
	$	$

Sunday

☐ ☐ ☐

	$	$
	$	$
	$	$
	$	$
	$	$
	$	$
	$	$
	$	$
	$	$
	$	$
	$	$

WEEKLY ESTIMATED

$ ____________

WEEKLY EXPENSES

$ ____________

=

MONTH OF:

Weekly Goal

WEEK -

HOW MUCH I WANT TO SAVE

$

ESTIMATED SPENDING MONEY

Monday

	$	$
	$	$
	$	$
	$	$
	$	$
	$	$
	$	$
	$	$
	$	$
	$	$
	$	$

Tuesday

	$	$
	$	$
	$	$
	$	$
	$	$
	$	$
	$	$
	$	$
	$	$
	$	$
	$	$

Wednesday

	$	$
	$	$
	$	$
	$	$
	$	$
	$	$
	$	$
	$	$
	$	$
	$	$
	$	$

Thursday

	$	$
	$	$
	$	$
	$	$
	$	$
	$	$
	$	$
	$	$
	$	$
	$	$
	$	$

MONTH OF:

Weekly Goal

WEEK -

ESTIMATED SPENDING MONEY

Friday

	$	$
	$	$
	$	$
	$	$
	$	$
	$	$
	$	$
	$	$
	$	$
	$	$
	$	$

Saturday

	$	$
	$	$
	$	$
	$	$
	$	$
	$	$
	$	$
	$	$
	$	$
	$	$
	$	$

Sunday

	$	$
	$	$
	$	$
	$	$
	$	$
	$	$
	$	$
	$	$
	$	$
	$	$
	$	$

WEEKLY ESTIMATED

$ __________

WEEKLY EXPENSES

$ __________

=

Weekly Savings

$ __________

Expense Tracker

DATE:	CATEGORY	AMOUNT
/ /		$
/ /		$
/ /		$
/ /		$
/ /		$
/ /		$
/ /		$
/ /		$
/ /		$
/ /		$
/ /		$
/ /		$
/ /		$
/ /		$
/ /		$
/ /		$
/ /		$
/ /		$
/ /		$
/ /		$
/ /		$
/ /		$
/ /		$
	TOTAL SPENDING	$

Monthly Balance Chart

TOTAL EXPENSES

CATEGORY

1. $ ____________
2. $ ____________
3. $ ____________
4. $ ____________

FIXED EXPENSES $ ____________

TOTAL EXPENSES $ ____________

SPENDING CIRCLE CHART

TOTAL INCOME $ ____________

TOTAL EXPENSES $ ____________

MONTHLY SAVE $ ____________

IMPORTANT NOTES

Special Notes

Kakeibo budget planner

MONTH OF: /

FAMILY ACCOUNT	SAVINGS ACCOUNT
Beginning of the Month $	Beginning of the Month $

INCOME

Date: / /	Details:	Amount $
Date: / /	Details:	Amount $
Date: / /	Details:	Amount $
Date: / /	Details:	Amount $
Date: / /	Details:	Amount $
Date: / /	Details:	Amount $

TOTAL AMOUNT: $

FIXED EXPENSES

Date: / /	Details:	Amount $
Date: / /	Details:	Amount $
Date: / /	Details:	Amount $
Date: / /	Details:	Amount $
Date: / /	Details:	Amount $
Date: / /	Details:	Amount $
Date: / /	Details:	Amount $
Date: / /	Details:	Amount $
Date: / /	Details:	Amount $
Date: / /	Details:	Amount $

TOTAL AMOUNT: $

AVAILABLE MONEY

$

MONTH OF:

Weekly Goal

WEEK -

HOW MUCH I WANT TO SAVE

$

ESTIMATED SPENDING MONEY

Monday

	$	$
	$	$
	$	$
	$	$
	$	$
	$	$
	$	$
	$	$
	$	$
	$	$
	$	$

Tuesday

	$	$
	$	$
	$	$
	$	$
	$	$
	$	$
	$	$
	$	$
	$	$
	$	$
	$	$

Wednesday

	$	$
	$	$
	$	$
	$	$
	$	$
	$	$
	$	$
	$	$
	$	$
	$	$
	$	$

Thursday

	$	$
	$	$
	$	$
	$	$
	$	$
	$	$
	$	$
	$	$
	$	$
	$	$
	$	$

MONTH OF:

Weekly Goal

WEEK -

ESTIMATED SPENDING MONEY

Friday

	$	$
	$	$
	$	$
	$	$
	$	$
	$	$
	$	$
	$	$
	$	$
	$	$
	$	$

Saturday

	$	$
	$	$
	$	$
	$	$
	$	$
	$	$
	$	$
	$	$
	$	$
	$	$
	$	$

Sunday

	$	$
	$	$
	$	$
	$	$
	$	$
	$	$
	$	$
	$	$
	$	$
	$	$
	$	$

WEEKLY ESTIMATED

$ ____________

WEEKLY EXPENSES

$ ____________

=

MONTH OF:

Weekly Goal

WEEK -

HOW MUCH I WANT TO SAVE

$

ESTIMATED SPENDING MONEY

Monday

	$	$
	$	$
	$	$
	$	$
	$	$
	$	$
	$	$
	$	$
	$	$
	$	$
	$	$

Tuesday

	$	$
	$	$
	$	$
	$	$
	$	$
	$	$
	$	$
	$	$
	$	$
	$	$
	$	$

Wednesday

	$	$
	$	$
	$	$
	$	$
	$	$
	$	$
	$	$
	$	$
	$	$
	$	$
	$	$

Thursday

	$	$
	$	$
	$	$
	$	$
	$	$
	$	$
	$	$
	$	$
	$	$
	$	$
	$	$

MONTH OF:

Weekly Goal

WEEK -

ESTIMATED SPENDING MONEY

Friday

	$	$
	$	$
	$	$
	$	$
	$	$
	$	$
	$	$
	$	$
	$	$
	$	$
	$	$

Saturday

	$	$
	$	$
	$	$
	$	$
	$	$
	$	$
	$	$
	$	$
	$	$
	$	$
	$	$

Sunday

	$	$
	$	$
	$	$
	$	$
	$	$
	$	$
	$	$
	$	$
	$	$
	$	$
	$	$

WEEKLY ESTIMATED

$ __________

WEEKLY EXPENSES

$ __________

=

MONTH OF:

Weekly Goal

WEEK -

HOW MUCH I WANT TO SAVE

$

ESTIMATED SPENDING MONEY

Monday

	$	$
	$	$
	$	$
	$	$
	$	$
	$	$
	$	$
	$	$
	$	$
	$	$
	$	$
	$	$

Tuesday

	$	$
	$	$
	$	$
	$	$
	$	$
	$	$
	$	$
	$	$
	$	$
	$	$
	$	$
	$	$

Wednesday

	$	$
	$	$
	$	$
	$	$
	$	$
	$	$
	$	$
	$	$
	$	$
	$	$
	$	$
	$	$

Thursday

	$	$
	$	$
	$	$
	$	$
	$	$
	$	$
	$	$
	$	$
	$	$
	$	$
	$	$
	$	$

MONTH OF:

Weekly Goal

WEEK -

ESTIMATED SPENDING MONEY

Friday

☐ ☐ ☐

	$	$
	$	$
	$	$
	$	$
	$	$
	$	$
	$	$
	$	$
	$	$
	$	$
	$	$

Saturday

☐ ☐ ☐

	$	$
	$	$
	$	$
	$	$
	$	$
	$	$
	$	$
	$	$
	$	$
	$	$
	$	$

Sunday

☐ ☐ ☐

	$	$
	$	$
	$	$
	$	$
	$	$
	$	$
	$	$
	$	$
	$	$
	$	$
	$	$

WEEKLY ESTIMATED

$ ____________

WEEKLY EXPENSES

$ ____________

=

Weekly Savings

$ ____________

MONTH OF:

Weekly Goal

WEEK -

HOW MUCH I WANT TO SAVE

$

ESTIMATED SPENDING MONEY

Monday

	$	$
	$	$
	$	$
	$	$
	$	$
	$	$
	$	$
	$	$
	$	$
	$	$
	$	$

Tuesday

	$	$
	$	$
	$	$
	$	$
	$	$
	$	$
	$	$
	$	$
	$	$
	$	$
	$	$

Wednesday

	$	$
	$	$
	$	$
	$	$
	$	$
	$	$
	$	$
	$	$
	$	$
	$	$
	$	$

Thursday

	$	$
	$	$
	$	$
	$	$
	$	$
	$	$
	$	$
	$	$
	$	$
	$	$
	$	$

MONTH OF:

Weekly Goal

WEEK -

ESTIMATED SPENDING MONEY

Friday

	$	$
	$	$
	$	$
	$	$
	$	$
	$	$
	$	$
	$	$
	$	$
	$	$
	$	$

Saturday

	$	$
	$	$
	$	$
	$	$
	$	$
	$	$
	$	$
	$	$
	$	$
	$	$
	$	$

Sunday

	$	$
	$	$
	$	$
	$	$
	$	$
	$	$
	$	$
	$	$
	$	$
	$	$
	$	$

WEEKLY ESTIMATED

$ ______

WEEKLY EXPENSES

$ ______

=

Expense Tracker

DATE:	CATEGORY	AMOUNT
/ /		$
/ /		$
/ /		$
/ /		$
/ /		$
/ /		$
/ /		$
/ /		$
/ /		$
/ /		$
/ /		$
/ /		$
/ /		$
/ /		$
/ /		$
/ /		$
/ /		$
/ /		$
/ /		$
/ /		$
/ /		$
/ /		$
/ /		$
	TOTAL SPENDING	$

Monthly Balance Chart

TOTAL EXPENSES

CATEGORY

1. $ ____________
2. $ ____________
3. $ ____________
4. $ ____________

FIXED EXPENSES $ ____________

TOTAL EXPENSES $ ____________

SPENDING CIRCLE CHART

TOTAL INCOME $ ____________

TOTAL EXPENSES $ ____________

MONTHLY SAVE $ ____________

IMPORTANT NOTES

- -

- -

- -

- -

- -

Special Notes

Kakeibo budget planner

MONTH OF: /

FAMILY ACCOUNT	SAVINGS ACCOUNT
Beginning of the Month $	Beginning of the Month $

INCOME

Date: / /	Details:	Amount $
Date: / /	Details:	Amount $
Date: / /	Details:	Amount $
Date: / /	Details:	Amount $
Date: / /	Details:	Amount $
Date: / /	Details:	Amount $

TOTAL AMOUNT: $

FIXED EXPENSES

Date: / /	Details:	Amount $
Date: / /	Details:	Amount $
Date: / /	Details:	Amount $
Date: / /	Details:	Amount $
Date: / /	Details:	Amount $
Date: / /	Details:	Amount $
Date: / /	Details:	Amount $
Date: / /	Details:	Amount $
Date: / /	Details:	Amount $
Date: / /	Details:	Amount $

TOTAL AMOUNT: $

AVAILABLE MONEY

$

MONTH OF:

Weekly Goal

WEEK -

HOW MUCH I WANT TO SAVE

$

ESTIMATED SPENDING MONEY

Monday

	$	$
	$	$
	$	$
	$	$
	$	$
	$	$
	$	$
	$	$
	$	$
	$	$
	$	$

Tuesday

	$	$
	$	$
	$	$
	$	$
	$	$
	$	$
	$	$
	$	$
	$	$
	$	$
	$	$

Wednesday

	$	$
	$	$
	$	$
	$	$
	$	$
	$	$
	$	$
	$	$
	$	$
	$	$
	$	$

Thursday

	$	$
	$	$
	$	$
	$	$
	$	$
	$	$
	$	$
	$	$
	$	$
	$	$
	$	$

MONTH OF:

Weekly Goal

WEEK -

ESTIMATED SPENDING MONEY

Friday

	$	$
	$	$
	$	$
	$	$
	$	$
	$	$
	$	$
	$	$
	$	$
	$	$
	$	$

Saturday

	$	$
	$	$
	$	$
	$	$
	$	$
	$	$
	$	$
	$	$
	$	$
	$	$
	$	$

Sunday

	$	$
	$	$
	$	$
	$	$
	$	$
	$	$
	$	$
	$	$
	$	$
	$	$
	$	$

WEEKLY ESTIMATED

$ ____________

WEEKLY EXPENSES

$ ____________

=

Weekly Savings

$ ____________

MONTH OF:

Weekly Goal

WEEK -

HOW MUCH I WANT TO SAVE

$

ESTIMATED SPENDING MONEY

Monday

	$	$
	$	$
	$	$
	$	$
	$	$
	$	$
	$	$
	$	$
	$	$
	$	$
	$	$

Tuesday

	$	$
	$	$
	$	$
	$	$
	$	$
	$	$
	$	$
	$	$
	$	$
	$	$
	$	$

Wednesday

	$	$
	$	$
	$	$
	$	$
	$	$
	$	$
	$	$
	$	$
	$	$
	$	$
	$	$

Thursday

	$	$
	$	$
	$	$
	$	$
	$	$
	$	$
	$	$
	$	$
	$	$
	$	$
	$	$

MONTH OF:

Weekly Goal

WEEK -

ESTIMATED SPENDING MONEY

Friday

	$	$
	$	$
	$	$
	$	$
	$	$
	$	$
	$	$
	$	$
	$	$
	$	$
	$	$

Saturday

	$	$
	$	$
	$	$
	$	$
	$	$
	$	$
	$	$
	$	$
	$	$
	$	$
	$	$

Sunday

	$	$
	$	$
	$	$
	$	$
	$	$
	$	$
	$	$
	$	$
	$	$
	$	$
	$	$

WEEKLY ESTIMATED

$ __________

WEEKLY EXPENSES

$ __________

=

MONTH OF:

Weekly Goal

WEEK -

HOW MUCH I WANT TO SAVE

$

ESTIMATED SPENDING MONEY

Monday

$ $
$ $
$ $
$ $
$ $
$ $
$ $
$ $
$ $
$ $
$ $

Tuesday

$ $
$ $
$ $
$ $
$ $
$ $
$ $
$ $
$ $
$ $
$ $

Wednesday

$ $
$ $
$ $
$ $
$ $
$ $
$ $
$ $
$ $
$ $
$ $

Thursday

$ $
$ $
$ $
$ $
$ $
$ $
$ $
$ $
$ $
$ $
$ $

MONTH OF:

Weekly Goal

WEEK -

ESTIMATED SPENDING MONEY

Friday

☐ ☐ ☐

	$	$
	$	$
	$	$
	$	$
	$	$
	$	$
	$	$
	$	$
	$	$
	$	$
	$	$

Saturday

☐ ☐ ☐

	$	$
	$	$
	$	$
	$	$
	$	$
	$	$
	$	$
	$	$
	$	$
	$	$
	$	$

Sunday

☐ ☐ ☐

	$	$
	$	$
	$	$
	$	$
	$	$
	$	$
	$	$
	$	$
	$	$
	$	$
	$	$

WEEKLY ESTIMATED

$ ____________

WEEKLY EXPENSES

$ ____________

=

Weekly Savings

$ ____________

MONTH OF:

Weekly Goal

WEEK -

HOW MUCH I WANT TO SAVE

$

ESTIMATED SPENDING MONEY

Monday

	$	$
	$	$
	$	$
	$	$
	$	$
	$	$
	$	$
	$	$
	$	$
	$	$
	$	$

Tuesday

	$	$
	$	$
	$	$
	$	$
	$	$
	$	$
	$	$
	$	$
	$	$
	$	$
	$	$

Wednesday

	$	$
	$	$
	$	$
	$	$
	$	$
	$	$
	$	$
	$	$
	$	$
	$	$
	$	$

Thursday

	$	$
	$	$
	$	$
	$	$
	$	$
	$	$
	$	$
	$	$
	$	$
	$	$
	$	$

MONTH OF:

Weekly Goal

WEEK -

ESTIMATED SPENDING MONEY

Friday

	$	$
	$	$
	$	$
	$	$
	$	$
	$	$
	$	$
	$	$
	$	$
	$	$
	$	$

Saturday

	$	$
	$	$
	$	$
	$	$
	$	$
	$	$
	$	$
	$	$
	$	$
	$	$
	$	$

Sunday

	$	$
	$	$
	$	$
	$	$
	$	$
	$	$
	$	$
	$	$
	$	$
	$	$
	$	$

WEEKLY ESTIMATED

$ ____________

WEEKLY EXPENSES

$ ____________

=

Weekly Savings

$ ____________

Expense Tracker

DATE:	CATEGORY	AMOUNT
/ /		$
/ /		$
/ /		$
/ /		$
/ /		$
/ /		$
/ /		$
/ /		$
/ /		$
/ /		$
/ /		$
/ /		$
/ /		$
/ /		$
/ /		$
/ /		$
/ /		$
/ /		$
/ /		$
/ /		$
/ /		$
/ /		$
/ /		$
	TOTAL SPENDING	$

Monthly Balance Chart

TOTAL EXPENSES

CATEGORY

1. $ ______
2. $ ______
3. $ ______
4. $ ______

FIXED EXPENSES $ ______

TOTAL EXPENSES $ ______

SPENDING CIRCLE CHART

TOTAL INCOME $ ______

TOTAL EXPENSES $ ______

MONTHLY SAVE $ ______

IMPORTANT NOTES

Special Notes

Kakeibo budget planner

MONTH OF: /

FAMILY ACCOUNT	SAVINGS ACCOUNT
Beginning of the Month $	Beginning of the Month $

INCOME

Date: / /	Details:	Amount $
Date: / /	Details:	Amount $
Date: / /	Details:	Amount $
Date: / /	Details:	Amount $
Date: / /	Details:	Amount $
Date: / /	Details:	Amount $

TOTAL AMOUNT: $

FIXED EXPENSES

Date: / /	Details:	Amount $
Date: / /	Details:	Amount $
Date: / /	Details:	Amount $
Date: / /	Details:	Amount $
Date: / /	Details:	Amount $
Date: / /	Details:	Amount $
Date: / /	Details:	Amount $
Date: / /	Details:	Amount $
Date: / /	Details:	Amount $
Date: / /	Details:	Amount $

TOTAL AMOUNT: $

AVAILABLE MONEY

$

MONTH OF:

Weekly Goal

WEEK -

HOW MUCH I WANT TO SAVE

$

ESTIMATED SPENDING MONEY

Monday

	$	$
	$	$
	$	$
	$	$
	$	$
	$	$
	$	$
	$	$
	$	$
	$	$
	$	$

Tuesday

	$	$
	$	$
	$	$
	$	$
	$	$
	$	$
	$	$
	$	$
	$	$
	$	$
	$	$

Wednesday

	$	$
	$	$
	$	$
	$	$
	$	$
	$	$
	$	$
	$	$
	$	$
	$	$
	$	$

Thursday

	$	$
	$	$
	$	$
	$	$
	$	$
	$	$
	$	$
	$	$
	$	$
	$	$
	$	$

MONTH OF:

Weekly Goal

WEEK -

ESTIMATED SPENDING MONEY

Friday

	$	$
	$	$
	$	$
	$	$
	$	$
	$	$
	$	$
	$	$
	$	$
	$	$
	$	$

Saturday

	$	$
	$	$
	$	$
	$	$
	$	$
	$	$
	$	$
	$	$
	$	$
	$	$
	$	$

Sunday

	$	$
	$	$
	$	$
	$	$
	$	$
	$	$
	$	$
	$	$
	$	$
	$	$
	$	$

WEEKLY ESTIMATED

$ ____________

WEEKLY EXPENSES

$ ____________

=

Weekly Savings

$ ____________

MONTH OF:

Weekly Goal

WEEK -

HOW MUCH I WANT TO SAVE

$

ESTIMATED SPENDING MONEY

Monday

	$	$
	$	$
	$	$
	$	$
	$	$
	$	$
	$	$
	$	$
	$	$
	$	$
	$	$

Tuesday

	$	$
	$	$
	$	$
	$	$
	$	$
	$	$
	$	$
	$	$
	$	$
	$	$
	$	$

Wednesday

	$	$
	$	$
	$	$
	$	$
	$	$
	$	$
	$	$
	$	$
	$	$
	$	$
	$	$

Thursday

	$	$
	$	$
	$	$
	$	$
	$	$
	$	$
	$	$
	$	$
	$	$
	$	$
	$	$

MONTH OF:

Weekly Goal

WEEK -

ESTIMATED SPENDING MONEY

Friday

☐ ☐ ☐

	$	$
	$	$
	$	$
	$	$
	$	$
	$	$
	$	$
	$	$
	$	$
	$	$
	$	$

Saturday

☐ ☐ ☐

	$	$
	$	$
	$	$
	$	$
	$	$
	$	$
	$	$
	$	$
	$	$
	$	$
	$	$

Sunday

☐ ☐ ☐

	$	$
	$	$
	$	$
	$	$
	$	$
	$	$
	$	$
	$	$
	$	$
	$	$
	$	$

WEEKLY ESTIMATED

$

WEEKLY EXPENSES

$

=

Weekly Savings

$

MONTH OF:

Weekly Goal

WEEK -

HOW MUCH I WANT TO SAVE

$

ESTIMATED SPENDING MONEY

Monday

	$	$
	$	$
	$	$
	$	$
	$	$
	$	$
	$	$
	$	$
	$	$
	$	$
	$	$

Tuesday

	$	$
	$	$
	$	$
	$	$
	$	$
	$	$
	$	$
	$	$
	$	$
	$	$
	$	$

Wednesday

	$	$
	$	$
	$	$
	$	$
	$	$
	$	$
	$	$
	$	$
	$	$
	$	$
	$	$

Thursday

	$	$
	$	$
	$	$
	$	$
	$	$
	$	$
	$	$
	$	$
	$	$
	$	$
	$	$

MONTH OF:

Weekly Goal

WEEK -

ESTIMATED SPENDING MONEY

Friday

	$	$
	$	$
	$	$
	$	$
	$	$
	$	$
	$	$
	$	$
	$	$
	$	$
	$	$

Saturday

	$	$
	$	$
	$	$
	$	$
	$	$
	$	$
	$	$
	$	$
	$	$
	$	$
	$	$

Sunday

	$	$
	$	$
	$	$
	$	$
	$	$
	$	$
	$	$
	$	$
	$	$
	$	$
	$	$

WEEKLY ESTIMATED

$ ____________

WEEKLY EXPENSES

$ ____________

=

Weekly Savings

$ ____________

MONTH OF:

Weekly Goal

WEEK -

HOW MUCH I WANT TO SAVE

$

ESTIMATED SPENDING MONEY

Monday

☐ ☐ ☐

	$	$
	$	$
	$	$
	$	$
	$	$
	$	$
	$	$
	$	$
	$	$
	$	$
	$	$

Tuesday

☐ ☐ ☐

	$	$
	$	$
	$	$
	$	$
	$	$
	$	$
	$	$
	$	$
	$	$
	$	$
	$	$

Wednesday

☐ ☐ ☐

	$	$
	$	$
	$	$
	$	$
	$	$
	$	$
	$	$
	$	$
	$	$
	$	$
	$	$

Thursday

☐ ☐ ☐

	$	$
	$	$
	$	$
	$	$
	$	$
	$	$
	$	$
	$	$
	$	$
	$	$
	$	$

MONTH OF:

Weekly Goal

WEEK -

ESTIMATED SPENDING MONEY

Friday

☹ ☺ ♥

	$	$
	$	$
	$	$
	$	$
	$	$
	$	$
	$	$
	$	$
	$	$
	$	$
	$	$

Saturday

☹ ☺ ♥

	$	$
	$	$
	$	$
	$	$
	$	$
	$	$
	$	$
	$	$
	$	$
	$	$
	$	$

Sunday

☹ ☺ ♥

	$	$
	$	$
	$	$
	$	$
	$	$
	$	$
	$	$
	$	$
	$	$
	$	$
	$	$

WEEKLY ESTIMATED

$ ____________

WEEKLY EXPENSES

$ ____________

=

Weekly Savings

$ ____________

Expense Tracker

DATE:	CATEGORY	AMOUNT
/ /		$
/ /		$
/ /		$
/ /		$
/ /		$
/ /		$
/ /		$
/ /		$
/ /		$
/ /		$
/ /		$
/ /		$
/ /		$
/ /		$
/ /		$
/ /		$
/ /		$
/ /		$
/ /		$
/ /		$
/ /		$
/ /		$
/ /		$
	TOTAL SPENDING	$

Monthly Balance Chart

TOTAL EXPENSES

CATEGORY	SPENDING CIRCLE CHART

1. $
2. $
3. $
4. $

FIXED EXPENSES $

TOTAL EXPENSES $

TOTAL INCOME $

TOTAL EXPENSES $

MONTHLY SAVE $

IMPORTANT NOTES

Special Notes

Kakeibo budget planner

MONTH OF: /

FAMILY ACCOUNT	SAVINGS ACCOUNT
Beginning of the Month $	Beginning of the Month $

INCOME

Date: / /	Details:	Amount $
Date: / /	Details:	Amount $
Date: / /	Details:	Amount $
Date: / /	Details:	Amount $
Date: / /	Details:	Amount $
Date: / /	Details:	Amount $

TOTAL AMOUNT: $

FIXED EXPENSES

Date: / /	Details:	Amount $
Date: / /	Details:	Amount $
Date: / /	Details:	Amount $
Date: / /	Details:	Amount $
Date: / /	Details:	Amount $
Date: / /	Details:	Amount $
Date: / /	Details:	Amount $
Date: / /	Details:	Amount $
Date: / /	Details:	Amount $
Date: / /	Details:	Amount $

TOTAL AMOUNT: $

AVAILABLE MONEY

$

MONTH OF:

Weekly Goal

WEEK -

HOW MUCH I WANT TO SAVE

$

ESTIMATED SPENDING MONEY

Monday

	$	$
	$	$
	$	$
	$	$
	$	$
	$	$
	$	$
	$	$
	$	$
	$	$
	$	$

Tuesday

	$	$
	$	$
	$	$
	$	$
	$	$
	$	$
	$	$
	$	$
	$	$
	$	$
	$	$

Wednesday

	$	$
	$	$
	$	$
	$	$
	$	$
	$	$
	$	$
	$	$
	$	$
	$	$
	$	$

Thursday

	$	$
	$	$
	$	$
	$	$
	$	$
	$	$
	$	$
	$	$
	$	$
	$	$
	$	$

MONTH OF:

Weekly Goal

WEEK -

ESTIMATED SPENDING MONEY

Friday

☐ ☐ ☐

	$	$
	$	$
	$	$
	$	$
	$	$
	$	$
	$	$
	$	$
	$	$
	$	$
	$	$

Saturday

☐ ☐ ☐

	$	$
	$	$
	$	$
	$	$
	$	$
	$	$
	$	$
	$	$
	$	$
	$	$
	$	$

Sunday

☐ ☐ ☐

	$	$
	$	$
	$	$
	$	$
	$	$
	$	$
	$	$
	$	$
	$	$
	$	$
	$	$

WEEKLY ESTIMATED

$ ____________

WEEKLY EXPENSES

$ ____________

=

Weekly Savings

$ ____________

MONTH OF:

Weekly Goal

WEEK -

HOW MUCH I WANT TO SAVE

$

ESTIMATED SPENDING MONEY

Monday

$ $
$ $
$ $
$ $
$ $
$ $
$ $
$ $
$ $
$ $
$ $

Tuesday

$ $
$ $
$ $
$ $
$ $
$ $
$ $
$ $
$ $
$ $
$ $

Wednesday

$ $
$ $
$ $
$ $
$ $
$ $
$ $
$ $
$ $
$ $
$ $

Thursday

$ $
$ $
$ $
$ $
$ $
$ $
$ $
$ $
$ $
$ $
$ $

MONTH OF:

Weekly Goal

WEEK -

ESTIMATED SPENDING MONEY

Friday

	$	$
	$	$
	$	$
	$	$
	$	$
	$	$
	$	$
	$	$
	$	$
	$	$
	$	$

Saturday

	$	$
	$	$
	$	$
	$	$
	$	$
	$	$
	$	$
	$	$
	$	$
	$	$
	$	$

Sunday

	$	$
	$	$
	$	$
	$	$
	$	$
	$	$
	$	$
	$	$
	$	$
	$	$
	$	$

WEEKLY ESTIMATED

$ ____________

WEEKLY EXPENSES

$ ____________

=

Weekly Savings

$ ____________

MONTH OF:

Weekly Goal

WEEK -

HOW MUCH I WANT TO SAVE

$

ESTIMATED SPENDING MONEY

Monday

	$	$
	$	$
	$	$
	$	$
	$	$
	$	$
	$	$
	$	$
	$	$
	$	$
	$	$

Tuesday

	$	$
	$	$
	$	$
	$	$
	$	$
	$	$
	$	$
	$	$
	$	$
	$	$
	$	$

Wednesday

	$	$
	$	$
	$	$
	$	$
	$	$
	$	$
	$	$
	$	$
	$	$
	$	$
	$	$

Thursday

	$	$
	$	$
	$	$
	$	$
	$	$
	$	$
	$	$
	$	$
	$	$
	$	$
	$	$

MONTH OF:

Weekly Goal

WEEK -

ESTIMATED SPENDING MONEY

Friday

☐ ☐ ☐

	$	$
	$	$
	$	$
	$	$
	$	$
	$	$
	$	$
	$	$
	$	$
	$	$
	$	$

Saturday

☐ ☐ ☐

	$	$
	$	$
	$	$
	$	$
	$	$
	$	$
	$	$
	$	$
	$	$
	$	$
	$	$

Sunday

☐ ☐ ☐

	$	$
	$	$
	$	$
	$	$
	$	$
	$	$
	$	$
	$	$
	$	$
	$	$
	$	$

WEEKLY ESTIMATED

$

WEEKLY EXPENSES

$

=

Weekly Savings

$

MONTH OF:

Weekly Goal

WEEK -

HOW MUCH I WANT TO SAVE

$

ESTIMATED SPENDING MONEY

Monday

	$	$
	$	$
	$	$
	$	$
	$	$
	$	$
	$	$
	$	$
	$	$
	$	$
	$	$

Tuesday

	$	$
	$	$
	$	$
	$	$
	$	$
	$	$
	$	$
	$	$
	$	$
	$	$
	$	$

Wednesday

	$	$
	$	$
	$	$
	$	$
	$	$
	$	$
	$	$
	$	$
	$	$
	$	$
	$	$

Thursday

	$	$
	$	$
	$	$
	$	$
	$	$
	$	$
	$	$
	$	$
	$	$
	$	$
	$	$

MONTH OF:

Weekly Goal

WEEK -

ESTIMATED SPENDING MONEY

Friday

	$	$
	$	$
	$	$
	$	$
	$	$
	$	$
	$	$
	$	$
	$	$
	$	$
	$	$

Saturday

	$	$
	$	$
	$	$
	$	$
	$	$
	$	$
	$	$
	$	$
	$	$
	$	$
	$	$

Sunday

	$	$
	$	$
	$	$
	$	$
	$	$
	$	$
	$	$
	$	$
	$	$
	$	$
	$	$

WEEKLY ESTIMATED

$ ____________

WEEKLY EXPENSES

$ ____________

=

Expense Tracker

DATE:	CATEGORY	AMOUNT
/ /		$
/ /		$
/ /		$
/ /		$
/ /		$
/ /		$
/ /		$
/ /		$
/ /		$
/ /		$
/ /		$
/ /		$
/ /		$
/ /		$
/ /		$
/ /		$
/ /		$
/ /		$
/ /		$
/ /		$
/ /		$
/ /		$
/ /		$
	TOTAL SPENDING	$

Monthly Balance Chart

TOTAL EXPENSES

CATEGORY

1. $
2. $
3. $
4. $

FIXED EXPENSES $

TOTAL EXPENSES $

SPENDING CIRCLE CHART

TOTAL INCOME $

TOTAL EXPENSES $

MONTHLY SAVE $

IMPORTANT NOTES

Special Notes

Kakeibo budget planner

MONTH OF: /

FAMILY ACCOUNT	SAVINGS ACCOUNT
Beginning of the Month $	Beginning of the Month $

INCOME

Date: / /	Details:	Amount $
Date: / /	Details:	Amount $
Date: / /	Details:	Amount $
Date: / /	Details:	Amount $
Date: / /	Details:	Amount $
Date: / /	Details:	Amount $

TOTAL AMOUNT: $

FIXED EXPENSES

Date: / /	Details:	Amount $
Date: / /	Details:	Amount $
Date: / /	Details:	Amount $
Date: / /	Details:	Amount $
Date: / /	Details:	Amount $
Date: / /	Details:	Amount $
Date: / /	Details:	Amount $
Date: / /	Details:	Amount $
Date: / /	Details:	Amount $
Date: / /	Details:	Amount $

TOTAL AMOUNT: $

AVAILABLE MONEY

$

MONTH OF:

Weekly Goal

WEEK -

HOW MUCH I WANT TO SAVE

$

ESTIMATED SPENDING MONEY

Monday

	$	$
	$	$
	$	$
	$	$
	$	$
	$	$
	$	$
	$	$
	$	$
	$	$
	$	$

Tuesday

	$	$
	$	$
	$	$
	$	$
	$	$
	$	$
	$	$
	$	$
	$	$
	$	$
	$	$

Wednesday

	$	$
	$	$
	$	$
	$	$
	$	$
	$	$
	$	$
	$	$
	$	$
	$	$
	$	$

Thursday

	$	$
	$	$
	$	$
	$	$
	$	$
	$	$
	$	$
	$	$
	$	$
	$	$
	$	$

MONTH OF:

Weekly Goal

WEEK -

ESTIMATED SPENDING MONEY

Friday

	$	$
	$	$
	$	$
	$	$
	$	$
	$	$
	$	$
	$	$
	$	$
	$	$
	$	$

Saturday

	$	$
	$	$
	$	$
	$	$
	$	$
	$	$
	$	$
	$	$
	$	$
	$	$
	$	$

Sunday

	$	$
	$	$
	$	$
	$	$
	$	$
	$	$
	$	$
	$	$
	$	$
	$	$
	$	$

WEEKLY ESTIMATED

$

WEEKLY EXPENSES

$

=

MONTH OF:

Weekly Goal

WEEK -

HOW MUCH I WANT TO SAVE

$

ESTIMATED SPENDING MONEY

Monday

	$	$
	$	$
	$	$
	$	$
	$	$
	$	$
	$	$
	$	$
	$	$
	$	$
	$	$

Tuesday

	$	$
	$	$
	$	$
	$	$
	$	$
	$	$
	$	$
	$	$
	$	$
	$	$
	$	$

Wednesday

	$	$
	$	$
	$	$
	$	$
	$	$
	$	$
	$	$
	$	$
	$	$
	$	$
	$	$

Thursday

	$	$
	$	$
	$	$
	$	$
	$	$
	$	$
	$	$
	$	$
	$	$
	$	$
	$	$

MONTH OF:

Weekly Goal

WEEK -

ESTIMATED SPENDING MONEY

Friday

☐ ☐ ☐

	$	$
	$	$
	$	$
	$	$
	$	$
	$	$
	$	$
	$	$
	$	$
	$	$
	$	$

Saturday

☐ ☐ ☐

	$	$
	$	$
	$	$
	$	$
	$	$
	$	$
	$	$
	$	$
	$	$
	$	$
	$	$

Sunday

☐ ☐ ☐

	$	$
	$	$
	$	$
	$	$
	$	$
	$	$
	$	$
	$	$
	$	$
	$	$
	$	$

WEEKLY ESTIMATED

$

WEEKLY EXPENSES

$

=

MONTH OF:

Weekly Goal

WEEK -

HOW MUCH I WANT TO SAVE

$

ESTIMATED SPENDING MONEY

Monday

	$	$
	$	$
	$	$
	$	$
	$	$
	$	$
	$	$
	$	$
	$	$
	$	$
	$	$

Tuesday

	$	$
	$	$
	$	$
	$	$
	$	$
	$	$
	$	$
	$	$
	$	$
	$	$
	$	$

Wednesday

	$	$
	$	$
	$	$
	$	$
	$	$
	$	$
	$	$
	$	$
	$	$
	$	$
	$	$

Thursday

	$	$
	$	$
	$	$
	$	$
	$	$
	$	$
	$	$
	$	$
	$	$
	$	$
	$	$

MONTH OF:

Weekly Goal

WEEK -

ESTIMATED SPENDING MONEY

Friday

	$	$
	$	$
	$	$
	$	$
	$	$
	$	$
	$	$
	$	$
	$	$
	$	$
	$	$

Saturday

	$	$
	$	$
	$	$
	$	$
	$	$
	$	$
	$	$
	$	$
	$	$
	$	$
	$	$

Sunday

	$	$
	$	$
	$	$
	$	$
	$	$
	$	$
	$	$
	$	$
	$	$
	$	$
	$	$

WEEKLY ESTIMATED

$ __________

WEEKLY EXPENSES

$ __________

=

MONTH OF:

Weekly Goal

WEEK -

HOW MUCH I WANT TO SAVE

$

ESTIMATED SPENDING MONEY

Monday

	$	$
	$	$
	$	$
	$	$
	$	$
	$	$
	$	$
	$	$
	$	$
	$	$
	$	$

Tuesday

	$	$
	$	$
	$	$
	$	$
	$	$
	$	$
	$	$
	$	$
	$	$
	$	$
	$	$

Wednesday

	$	$
	$	$
	$	$
	$	$
	$	$
	$	$
	$	$
	$	$
	$	$
	$	$
	$	$

Thursday

	$	$
	$	$
	$	$
	$	$
	$	$
	$	$
	$	$
	$	$
	$	$
	$	$
	$	$

MONTH OF:

Weekly Goal

WEEK -

ESTIMATED SPENDING MONEY

Friday

	$	$
	$	$
	$	$
	$	$
	$	$
	$	$
	$	$
	$	$
	$	$
	$	$
	$	$

Saturday

	$	$
	$	$
	$	$
	$	$
	$	$
	$	$
	$	$
	$	$
	$	$
	$	$
	$	$

Sunday

	$	$
	$	$
	$	$
	$	$
	$	$
	$	$
	$	$
	$	$
	$	$
	$	$
	$	$

WEEKLY ESTIMATED

$ ____________

WEEKLY EXPENSES

$ ____________

=

Weekly Savings

$ ____________

Expense Tracker

DATE:	CATEGORY	AMOUNT
/ /		$
/ /		$
/ /		$
/ /		$
/ /		$
/ /		$
/ /		$
/ /		$
/ /		$
/ /		$
/ /		$
/ /		$
/ /		$
/ /		$
/ /		$
/ /		$
/ /		$
/ /		$
/ /		$
/ /		$
/ /		$
/ /		$
/ /		$
	TOTAL SPENDING	$

Monthly Balance Chart

TOTAL EXPENSES

CATEGORY	SPENDING CIRCLE CHART

1. $
2. $
3. $
4. $

FIXED EXPENSES $

TOTAL EXPENSES $

TOTAL INCOME $

TOTAL EXPENSES $

MONTHLY SAVE $

IMPORTANT NOTES

Special Notes

Kakeibo budget planner

MONTH OF: /

FAMILY ACCOUNT	SAVINGS ACCOUNT
Beginning of the Month $	Beginning of the Month $

INCOME

Date: / /	Details:	Amount $
Date: / /	Details:	Amount $
Date: / /	Details:	Amount $
Date: / /	Details:	Amount $
Date: / /	Details:	Amount $
Date: / /	Details:	Amount $

TOTAL AMOUNT: $

FIXED EXPENSES

Date: / /	Details:	Amount $
Date: / /	Details:	Amount $
Date: / /	Details:	Amount $
Date: / /	Details:	Amount $
Date: / /	Details:	Amount $
Date: / /	Details:	Amount $
Date: / /	Details:	Amount $
Date: / /	Details:	Amount $
Date: / /	Details:	Amount $
Date: / /	Details:	Amount $

TOTAL AMOUNT: $

AVAILABLE MONEY

$

MONTH OF:

Weekly Goal

WEEK -

HOW MUCH I WANT TO SAVE

$

ESTIMATED SPENDING MONEY

Monday

☐ ☐ ☐

	$	$
	$	$
	$	$
	$	$
	$	$
	$	$
	$	$
	$	$
	$	$
	$	$
	$	$

Tuesday

☐ ☐ ☐

	$	$
	$	$
	$	$
	$	$
	$	$
	$	$
	$	$
	$	$
	$	$
	$	$
	$	$

Wednesday

☐ ☐ ☐

	$	$
	$	$
	$	$
	$	$
	$	$
	$	$
	$	$
	$	$
	$	$
	$	$
	$	$

Thursday

☐ ☐ ☐

	$	$
	$	$
	$	$
	$	$
	$	$
	$	$
	$	$
	$	$
	$	$
	$	$
	$	$

MONTH OF:

Weekly Goal

WEEK -

ESTIMATED SPENDING MONEY

Friday

	$	$
	$	$
	$	$
	$	$
	$	$
	$	$
	$	$
	$	$
	$	$
	$	$
	$	$

Saturday

	$	$
	$	$
	$	$
	$	$
	$	$
	$	$
	$	$
	$	$
	$	$
	$	$
	$	$

Sunday

	$	$
	$	$
	$	$
	$	$
	$	$
	$	$
	$	$
	$	$
	$	$
	$	$
	$	$

WEEKLY ESTIMATED

$ ____________

WEEKLY EXPENSES

$ ____________

=

MONTH OF:

Weekly Goal

WEEK -

HOW MUCH I WANT TO SAVE

$

ESTIMATED SPENDING MONEY

Monday

	$	$
	$	$
	$	$
	$	$
	$	$
	$	$
	$	$
	$	$
	$	$
	$	$
	$	$

Tuesday

	$	$
	$	$
	$	$
	$	$
	$	$
	$	$
	$	$
	$	$
	$	$
	$	$
	$	$

Wednesday

	$	$
	$	$
	$	$
	$	$
	$	$
	$	$
	$	$
	$	$
	$	$
	$	$
	$	$

Thursday

	$	$
	$	$
	$	$
	$	$
	$	$
	$	$
	$	$
	$	$
	$	$
	$	$
	$	$

MONTH OF:

Weekly Goal

WEEK -

ESTIMATED SPENDING MONEY

Friday

☐ ☐ ☐

	$	$
	$	$
	$	$
	$	$
	$	$
	$	$
	$	$
	$	$
	$	$
	$	$
	$	$

Saturday

☐ ☐ ☐

	$	$
	$	$
	$	$
	$	$
	$	$
	$	$
	$	$
	$	$
	$	$
	$	$
	$	$

Sunday

☐ ☐ ☐

	$	$
	$	$
	$	$
	$	$
	$	$
	$	$
	$	$
	$	$
	$	$
	$	$
	$	$

WEEKLY ESTIMATED

$ ________

WEEKLY EXPENSES

$ ________

=

Weekly Savings

$ ________

MONTH OF:

Weekly Goal

WEEK -

HOW MUCH I WANT TO SAVE

$

ESTIMATED SPENDING MONEY

Monday

	$	$
	$	$
	$	$
	$	$
	$	$
	$	$
	$	$
	$	$
	$	$
	$	$
	$	$

Tuesday

	$	$
	$	$
	$	$
	$	$
	$	$
	$	$
	$	$
	$	$
	$	$
	$	$
	$	$

Wednesday

	$	$
	$	$
	$	$
	$	$
	$	$
	$	$
	$	$
	$	$
	$	$
	$	$
	$	$

Thursday

	$	$
	$	$
	$	$
	$	$
	$	$
	$	$
	$	$
	$	$
	$	$
	$	$
	$	$

MONTH OF:

Weekly Goal

WEEK -

ESTIMATED SPENDING MONEY

Friday

$ $
$ $
$ $
$ $
$ $
$ $
$ $
$ $
$ $
$ $
$ $

Saturday

$ $
$ $
$ $
$ $
$ $
$ $
$ $
$ $
$ $
$ $
$ $

Sunday

$ $
$ $
$ $
$ $
$ $
$ $
$ $
$ $
$ $
$ $
$ $

WEEKLY ESTIMATED

$

WEEKLY EXPENSES

$

=

Weekly Savings

$

MONTH OF:

Weekly Goal

WEEK -

HOW MUCH I WANT TO SAVE

$

ESTIMATED SPENDING MONEY

Monday

	$	$
	$	$
	$	$
	$	$
	$	$
	$	$
	$	$
	$	$
	$	$
	$	$
	$	$

Tuesday

	$	$
	$	$
	$	$
	$	$
	$	$
	$	$
	$	$
	$	$
	$	$
	$	$
	$	$

Wednesday

	$	$
	$	$
	$	$
	$	$
	$	$
	$	$
	$	$
	$	$
	$	$
	$	$
	$	$

Thursday

	$	$
	$	$
	$	$
	$	$
	$	$
	$	$
	$	$
	$	$
	$	$
	$	$
	$	$

MONTH OF:

Weekly Goal

WEEK -

ESTIMATED SPENDING MONEY

Friday

	$	$
	$	$
	$	$
	$	$
	$	$
	$	$
	$	$
	$	$
	$	$
	$	$
	$	$

Saturday

	$	$
	$	$
	$	$
	$	$
	$	$
	$	$
	$	$
	$	$
	$	$
	$	$
	$	$

Sunday

	$	$
	$	$
	$	$
	$	$
	$	$
	$	$
	$	$
	$	$
	$	$
	$	$
	$	$

WEEKLY ESTIMATED

$

WEEKLY EXPENSES

$

=

Expense Tracker

DATE:	CATEGORY	AMOUNT
/ /		$
/ /		$
/ /		$
/ /		$
/ /		$
/ /		$
/ /		$
/ /		$
/ /		$
/ /		$
/ /		$
/ /		$
/ /		$
/ /		$
/ /		$
/ /		$
/ /		$
/ /		$
/ /		$
/ /		$
/ /		$
/ /		$
/ /		$
	TOTAL SPENDING	$

Monthly Balance Chart

TOTAL EXPENSES

CATEGORY	SPENDING CIRCLE CHART

1. $ __________
2. $ __________
3. $ __________
4. $ __________

FIXED EXPENSES $ __________

TOTAL EXPENSES $ __________

TOTAL INCOME $ __________

TOTAL EXPENSES $ __________

MONTHLY SAVE $ __________

IMPORTANT NOTES

Special Notes

Kakeibo budget planner

MONTH OF: /

FAMILY ACCOUNT	SAVINGS ACCOUNT
Beginning of the Month $	Beginning of the Month $

INCOME

Date: / /	Details:	Amount $
Date: / /	Details:	Amount $
Date: / /	Details:	Amount $
Date: / /	Details:	Amount $
Date: / /	Details:	Amount $
Date: / /	Details:	Amount $

TOTAL AMOUNT: $

FIXED EXPENSES

Date: / /	Details:	Amount $
Date: / /	Details:	Amount $
Date: / /	Details:	Amount $
Date: / /	Details:	Amount $
Date: / /	Details:	Amount $
Date: / /	Details:	Amount $
Date: / /	Details:	Amount $
Date: / /	Details:	Amount $
Date: / /	Details:	Amount $
Date: / /	Details:	Amount $

TOTAL AMOUNT: $

AVAILABLE MONEY

$

MONTH OF:

Weekly Goal

WEEK -

HOW MUCH I WANT TO SAVE

$

ESTIMATED SPENDING MONEY

Monday

	$	$
	$	$
	$	$
	$	$
	$	$
	$	$
	$	$
	$	$
	$	$
	$	$
	$	$

Tuesday

	$	$
	$	$
	$	$
	$	$
	$	$
	$	$
	$	$
	$	$
	$	$
	$	$
	$	$

Wednesday

	$	$
	$	$
	$	$
	$	$
	$	$
	$	$
	$	$
	$	$
	$	$
	$	$
	$	$

Thursday

	$	$
	$	$
	$	$
	$	$
	$	$
	$	$
	$	$
	$	$
	$	$
	$	$
	$	$

MONTH OF:

Weekly Goal

WEEK -

ESTIMATED SPENDING MONEY

Friday

	$	$
	$	$
	$	$
	$	$
	$	$
	$	$
	$	$
	$	$
	$	$
	$	$
	$	$

Saturday

	$	$
	$	$
	$	$
	$	$
	$	$
	$	$
	$	$
	$	$
	$	$
	$	$
	$	$

Sunday

	$	$
	$	$
	$	$
	$	$
	$	$
	$	$
	$	$
	$	$
	$	$
	$	$
	$	$

WEEKLY ESTIMATED

$ ____________

WEEKLY EXPENSES

$ ____________

=

MONTH OF:

Weekly Goal

WEEK -

HOW MUCH I WANT TO SAVE

$

ESTIMATED SPENDING MONEY

Monday

	$	$
	$	$
	$	$
	$	$
	$	$
	$	$
	$	$
	$	$
	$	$
	$	$
	$	$

Tuesday

	$	$
	$	$
	$	$
	$	$
	$	$
	$	$
	$	$
	$	$
	$	$
	$	$
	$	$

Wednesday

	$	$
	$	$
	$	$
	$	$
	$	$
	$	$
	$	$
	$	$
	$	$
	$	$
	$	$

Thursday

	$	$
	$	$
	$	$
	$	$
	$	$
	$	$
	$	$
	$	$
	$	$
	$	$
	$	$

MONTH OF:

Weekly Goal

WEEK -

ESTIMATED SPENDING MONEY

Friday

☐ ☐ ☐

	$	$
	$	$
	$	$
	$	$
	$	$
	$	$
	$	$
	$	$
	$	$
	$	$
	$	$

Saturday

☐ ☐ ☐

	$	$
	$	$
	$	$
	$	$
	$	$
	$	$
	$	$
	$	$
	$	$
	$	$
	$	$

Sunday

☐ ☐ ☐

	$	$
	$	$
	$	$
	$	$
	$	$
	$	$
	$	$
	$	$
	$	$
	$	$
	$	$

WEEKLY ESTIMATED

$ __________

WEEKLY EXPENSES

$ __________

=

Weekly Savings

$ __________

MONTH OF:

Weekly Goal

WEEK -

HOW MUCH I WANT TO SAVE

$

ESTIMATED SPENDING MONEY

Monday

	$	$
	$	$
	$	$
	$	$
	$	$
	$	$
	$	$
	$	$
	$	$
	$	$
	$	$

Tuesday

	$	$
	$	$
	$	$
	$	$
	$	$
	$	$
	$	$
	$	$
	$	$
	$	$
	$	$

Wednesday

	$	$
	$	$
	$	$
	$	$
	$	$
	$	$
	$	$
	$	$
	$	$
	$	$
	$	$

Thursday

	$	$
	$	$
	$	$
	$	$
	$	$
	$	$
	$	$
	$	$
	$	$
	$	$
	$	$

MONTH OF:

Weekly Goal

WEEK -

ESTIMATED SPENDING MONEY

Friday

	$	$
	$	$
	$	$
	$	$
	$	$
	$	$
	$	$
	$	$
	$	$
	$	$
	$	$

Saturday

	$	$
	$	$
	$	$
	$	$
	$	$
	$	$
	$	$
	$	$
	$	$
	$	$
	$	$

Sunday

	$	$
	$	$
	$	$
	$	$
	$	$
	$	$
	$	$
	$	$
	$	$
	$	$
	$	$

WEEKLY ESTIMATED

$ ____________

WEEKLY EXPENSES

$ ____________

=

Weekly Savings

$ ____________

MONTH OF:

Weekly Goal

WEEK -

HOW MUCH I WANT TO SAVE

$

ESTIMATED SPENDING MONEY

Monday

	$	$
	$	$
	$	$
	$	$
	$	$
	$	$
	$	$
	$	$
	$	$
	$	$
	$	$

Tuesday

	$	$
	$	$
	$	$
	$	$
	$	$
	$	$
	$	$
	$	$
	$	$
	$	$
	$	$

Wednesday

	$	$
	$	$
	$	$
	$	$
	$	$
	$	$
	$	$
	$	$
	$	$
	$	$
	$	$

Thursday

	$	$
	$	$
	$	$
	$	$
	$	$
	$	$
	$	$
	$	$
	$	$
	$	$
	$	$

MONTH OF:

Weekly Goal

WEEK -

ESTIMATED SPENDING MONEY

Friday

☐ ☐ ☐

	$	$
	$	$
	$	$
	$	$
	$	$
	$	$
	$	$
	$	$
	$	$
	$	$
	$	$

Saturday

☐ ☐ ☐

	$	$
	$	$
	$	$
	$	$
	$	$
	$	$
	$	$
	$	$
	$	$
	$	$
	$	$

Sunday

☐ ☐ ☐

	$	$
	$	$
	$	$
	$	$
	$	$
	$	$
	$	$
	$	$
	$	$
	$	$
	$	$

WEEKLY ESTIMATED

$ ____________

WEEKLY EXPENSES

$ ____________

=

Expense Tracker

DATE:	CATEGORY	AMOUNT
/ /		$
/ /		$
/ /		$
/ /		$
/ /		$
/ /		$
/ /		$
/ /		$
/ /		$
/ /		$
/ /		$
/ /		$
/ /		$
/ /		$
/ /		$
/ /		$
/ /		$
/ /		$
/ /		$
/ /		$
/ /		$
/ /		$
/ /		$
	TOTAL SPENDING	$

Monthly Balance Chart

TOTAL EXPENSES

CATEGORY

1. $ ____________
2. $ ____________
3. $ ____________
4. $ ____________

FIXED EXPENSES $ ____________

TOTAL EXPENSES $ ____________

SPENDING CIRCLE CHART

TOTAL INCOME $ ____________

TOTAL EXPENSES $ ____________

MONTHLY SAVE $ ____________

IMPORTANT NOTES

Special Notes

Anual Revenues & Expenses

MONTH	INCOME	EXPENSES
	$	$
	$	$
	$	$
	$	$
	$	$
	$	$
	$	$
	$	$
	$	$
	$	$
	$	$
	$	$
TOTAL	**$**	**$**

Special Notes

Made in the USA
Monee, IL
04 November 2026

67385522R00085